THE SUPERSTAR IN YOU!

written by
Keirsten Wanamaker

Illustrated by
Jasmine Hatcher

Watersprings
PUBLISHING

Published by Watersprings Publishing, a division of
Watersprings Media House, LLC.
P.O. BOX 1284
Olive Branch, MS 38654
www.waterspringsmedia.com
Contact publisher for bulk orders and permission requests.

Printed in the United States of America.

ISBN-13: 978-1-948877-57-2

I want to dedicate this book to
my family, Henry, Jason, Corey, and
my parents for always encouraging me.

To all the beautiful children of color
on this Earth...Keep shining!

Two of the most important words in the English language are "I am".
When you say positive words after "I am", you are creating who you will
be. What you say you are can either make you happy or unhappy.
We were all put on this Earth with a special gift.

When you speak positive words about yourself and do your best, you can
be, do, and have whatever you want in your life!

Always remember, you are a star! God made you and you were made
perfect. There is no one else like you.
When someone asks, "who are you?'
Smile and then tell them...

I AM SMART

I love to learn, and I make good decisions.

I AM CREATIVE

I have a curious mind
and I'm filled with
great ideas.

I AM BEAUTIFUL

My inside and my
outside are attractive.

I AM A WINNER

I work hard, and I never quit.

I AM AWESOME

I have a positive attitude,
and people trust me.

I AM TALENTED

I use my gifts and I share them.

I AM UNIQUE

I have a special personality,
and there is no one else like me.

I AM GOOD

I love helping people, and I care for others.

I AM BLESSED

I have all that I need to
live an amazing life.

I AM SPECIAL

I deserve great things and I let others know they are special too.

I AM SUCCESSFUL

I love to learn, and I get better every day.

I AM STRONG

I know how to control my emotions,
and I know right from wrong.

I AM ENOUGH

I love who I am, and I don't try to be like anyone else.

I AM HAPPY

I appreciate everything I have
and I have faith in my abilities.

I AM HEALTHY

I only allow good things into
my body and mind.

I AM FUN

I like to try new things with my family and friends.

I AM BRAVE

I face difficult situations with courage and overcome fears with ease.

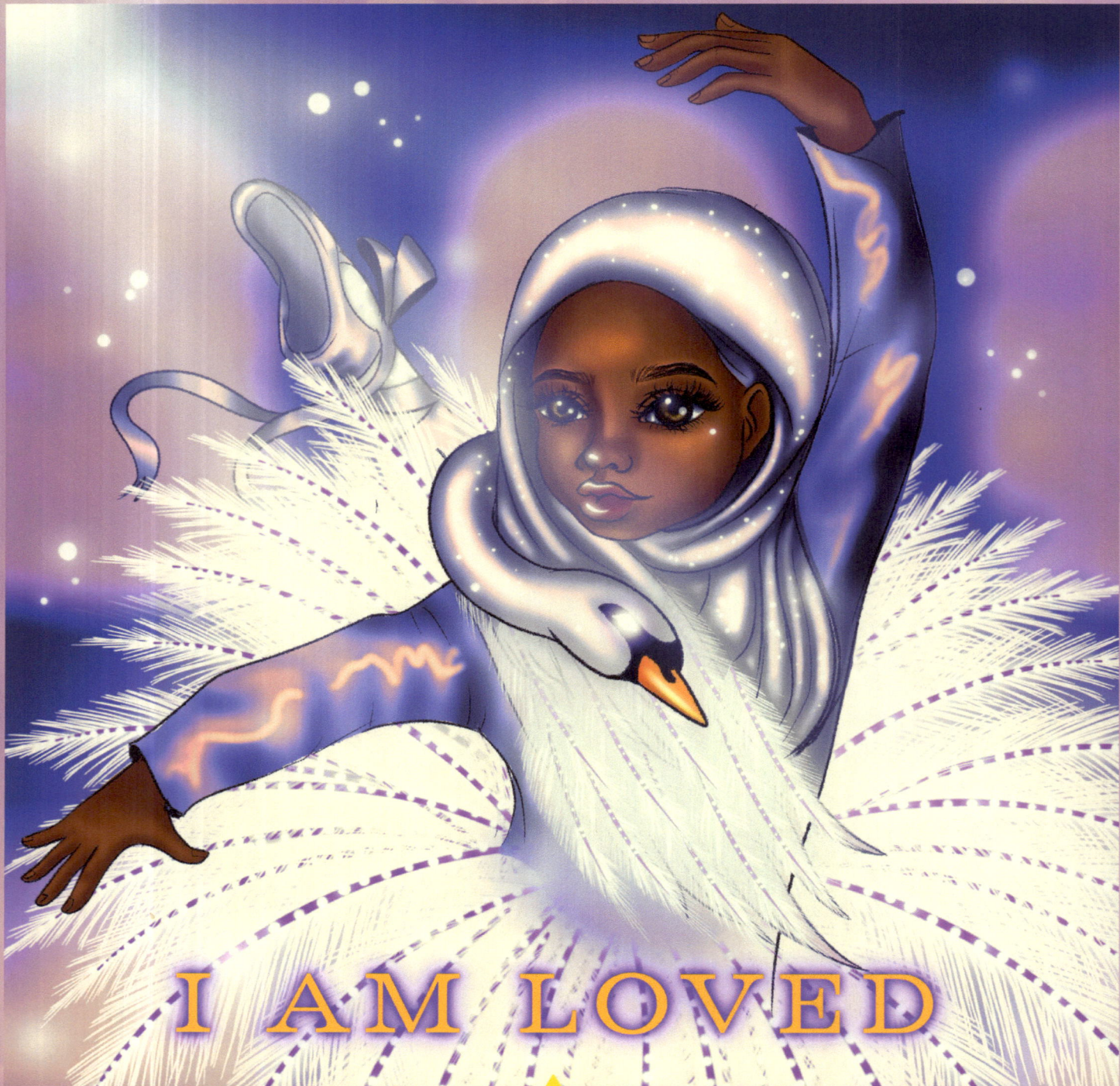

I AM LOVED

I love who I am,
and others love me too.

I AM A LEADER

I inspire others, and I am a good communicator.

I AM IMPORTANT

I contribute to my community
and motivate people.

I AM IN CONTROL

I know how to stay calm and relaxed when I'm afraid.

I AM MAGICAL

I believe I can make all of my dreams come true.

I AM GRATEFUL

I have a lot in my life to be thankful for.

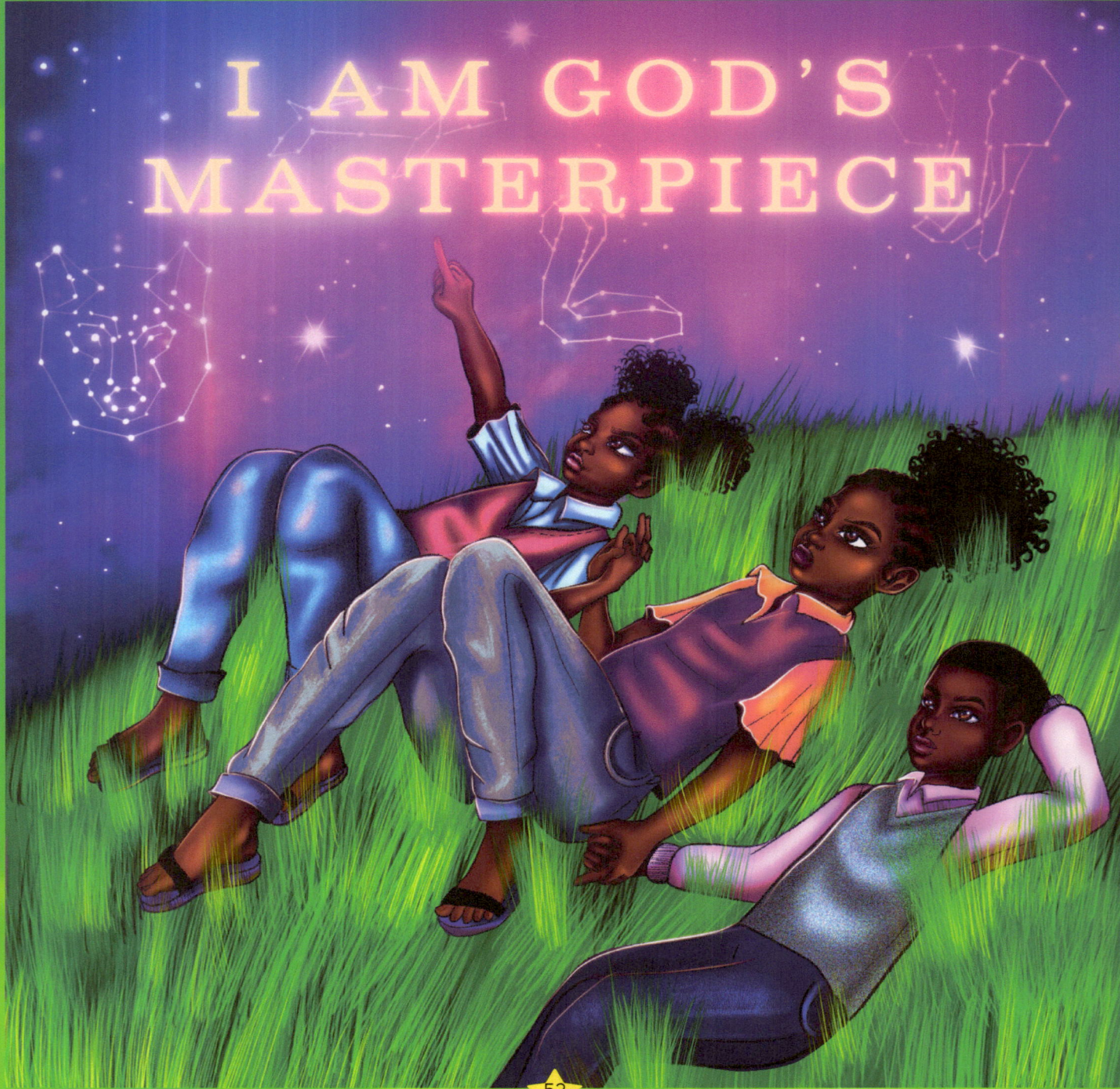

I AM GOD'S MASTERPIECE

God made me,
and I am a blessing!

*Special thanks
to John Ostrosky for your creativity, talent, and
support during my writing process.*

ABOUT THE AUTHOR

Keirsten Wanamaker

Keirsten Wanamaker has worked in the children's television and photography industry for over 20 years. She earned her BA in Mass Media Communications from Hampton University in Virginia. She is passionate about health and wellness, and inspiring children and women to be their best selves. She lives in Westchester County, NY with her husband and two teenage boys.

www.ingramcontent.com/pod-product-compliance
Lightning Source LLC
Chambersburg PA
CBHW042007080426
42733CB00003B/30